✥ AN OBSERVER

Materials & Techniques of Oil Painting

☉ OBSERVER'S GUIDES

Home and Garden
The Herb Grower's Guide
Car Care

Art and Craft
Pencil Drawing
Drawing with Ink
Using Pastels
Beginning Watercolour
Materials and Techniques of Oil Painting
Materials and Techniques of Watercolour
Materials and Techniques of Acrylic Painting
Materials and Techniques of Collage
Let's Make Pottery
First Steps in Upholstery – Traditional Handmade

Where Is It?
British Paintings – Hogarth to Turner
European Paintings of the 18th Century
Twentieth Century Paintings – Bonnard to Rothko
Italian, French and Spanish Paintings of the 17th Century
Paintings and Sculpture of the 15th Century
Dutch and Flemish Paintings of the 17th Century
European Paintings of the 19th Century
British Paintings of the 19th Century

Materials & Techniques of Oil Painting

John FitzMaurice Mills

FREDERICK WARNE

Published by Frederick Warne (Publishers) Ltd, London, 1981

ISBN 0 7232 2472 2

Printed and bound in Great Britain by
William Clowes (Beccles) Limited, Beccles and London
1499.1180

Contents

Choice of colours and speed of drying. Media, diluents and solvents. Retouching varnish. Varnishes. Supports. Brushes. Knives. Palettes. Dippers. Mahl stick. Canvas pins. Easels. The studio. Daylight. Artificial light. Walls and ceiling. Floors. Heating. Painting table

Preparation of supports. Setting out the palette. Imprimatura. Colour mixing. Brushwork. Knife painting. Drawing in. Composition. Light. Pentimento. Underpainting. Overpainting. Alla prima. Impasto. Sgraffito. Glazing. Velatura. Scumbling. Rubbing. 'Tonking'. Varnishing. Framing

Foreword

The word 'oils' is evocative. It brings with it an image of the artist's studio, the aromatic scents of the materials, stretched canvases or prepared panels. The eye conjures up a beckoning landscape, an array of exquisite flowers, a patient model.

There is something about going along to the art shop and pondering over the display of colours in fat tubes, the racks of brushes, the lines of bottles and the rest. Then having made the purchase – back to savour them and take those first steps.

The buttery rich consistency of the colours as they are squeezed out on the palette urges on. The white or tinted face of the canvas on the easel may daunt at first. But approach that initial attack with joy and never yield to discouragement. Even if the first results may disappoint, no harm is done and they can be scrapped; at the least they will have done something to start building up that experience from which will grow the next step towards greater proficiency.

To stand or sit in front of an easel 'having a go' at a landscape, still life or other subject is like entering another world, temporarily eluding outside pressures. Paint on whilst the joy of the moment is with you. If this joy seems to wane, leave matters for the time and come back again later.

Oil painting terminology

Abbozzo   The first sketch or underpainting. It can also be termed dead colouring for the reason that some painters use monochrome at this stage.

Absorbed   During painting with oils on some grounds and supports, areas of some colours, very often the earths, dry out flat with a lifeless dull surface; the reason for this being that the vehicle has been absorbed into the priming.

Absorbent grounds   Where plaster or gesso grounds (see p. 32) are made up without oil they will be highly absorbent of not only oil but also water. If an oil painting is to be done on such a ground, it will be impermanent, as the binder will be leached out and the paint will be likely to flake off. For permanence, it is essential that the ground is thoroughly isolated. This can be done by brushing over with size or, better still, by using shellac dissolved to saturation point in alcohol (see p. 32).

Academy board   An economical support for oils. It was introduced in the nineteenth century. Generally a pasteboard about 3 mm ($\frac{1}{8}$ in) thick, white lead primed on one side and pale grey on the reverse.

Achromatic colours   Black, white and greys as opposed to the other colours – the chromatics.

Adherence   Referring to paint films, it is their ability to remain permanently on the support. Oils will hold well on correctly primed surfaces, but will be weak on absorbent non-isolated grounds, and non-absorbent highly polished surfaces such as glass and metal.

Alkyd   A name derived from 'alcid', a word coined in 1927 to indicate a substance made from alcohols and acids. From the wide range of alkyd resins developed over the years an oil-modified variety has proved a satisfactory vehicle for pigments, and a range of colours for the artist that has a number of distinct advantages has been manufactured. The alkyd colours all dry at the same speed, reaching 'skin-dry' in about eighteen hours (see p. 21). They are eminently suited for glazing. These colours can be diluted with turpentine or white spirit and all the media compatible with traditional oils. Further, they can be used in conjunction with oil colours, wet in wet or as an underpainting (p. 49) or overpainting (p. 50).

Alligator cracks   The irregular crack patterns that can appear in some paint films if the colours, particularly the dark earths, have been unwisely thinned or applied. Some of the older natural resin varnishes will also crack in this manner, especially if the picture has been varnished before the paint is properly dried out; this is caused by opposing movements in the paint and the varnish films.

Asphaltum   Also known as bitumen. A dark warm brown, usually with a crimson tinge. It was extensively used as a pigment in the late eighteenth century and during the nineteenth century. The substance was dissolved in linseed oil or turpentine and either mixed in with other colours or used extensively for glazing. It will bleed into neighbouring colours; but worse, it forms heavy areas of deep cracking and hard lumps, at times up to 3 mm ($\frac{1}{8}$ in) thick. A picture that has been painted with large quantities of asphaltum can be difficult to restore because the slightest touch with even a weak solvent on the varnish can almost at once dissolve the underlying paint.

Back-glass painting   A manner of working which was once in vogue, but which is little practised today. The method implies painting on the back of a sheet of glass. The glass must be meticulously clean and quite dry. The painter then works in reverse, putting down the normal finishing strokes first; i.e., the lights in the eyes, highlights and any strong accents in the foreground. He then works his way backwards. The colours show up with maximum brilliance and the method has considerable permanence, as the pigments and their vehicle are imprisoned behind the glass and cannot be affected by the atmosphere or pollutants. It is general practice to seal in the back with a sheet of metal foil.

Backing   Some form of protective covering for the back of an oil-painting support. This may be paint, wax, metal foil, or a sheet of a material such as hardboard.

Binder   The holding ingredient in the vehicle mixed with the pigments. The purpose of the binder is to hold the pigment particles in place so as to form an even dispersion and cause them to adhere firmly to the support.

Blisters   If an oil on canvas or on a panel becomes damp the moisture will attack the size or priming and cause these to swell. In turn the paint will come away in either round blisters or long ridges similar to small mountain ranges. When noticed this condition should be treated by a professional restorer as soon as possible.

Bloom   A grey-white mist that can come up on the varnish of a picture, often over the darker colours, particularly the earths. It may be caused by damp conditions when varnishing or damp and cold in its hanging position. Also called blanch and chill.

Broken colour   A term that was first used by the French Impressionists in the nineteenth century. It is the application of the colours interspersed one with another using short hatching and sometimes completely separated strokes. The effect created is largely an optical mixture; for example, yellow and red strokes viewed from a short way away come up as orange.

Camaieu   A manner of painting in monochrome, the whole being produced in tones from one colour and being varied by the play of light and shade. It may also be applied to a painting that is composed of a number of tints which do not copy the natural colours.

Canvas board   A cheap oil support where a low grade canvas is glued to a stiff cardboard. The surface is then primed in the normal way. A wide variety of fabrics can be used, but it should be borne in mind that the support by its nature will not have great permanence. If the canvas boards are too large they will be prone to warping and will need supporting battens.

Cleavage   The term for the separation of various layers of an oil painting – the priming, the paint films and the varnish. It is normally caused by faulty practice in the preparation of the support, the application of the paint or the varnish.

Colour circle   A circular arrangement of the primary, secondary and tertiary colours. The French Impressionists worked broadly from the simplest circle. Here the colours read clockwise as yellow, orange, red, violet, blue and green. Painters working from this will get the maximum effect by putting down colours next to each other that are on opposing sides of the circle; thus, red next to green, orange next to blue, and violet next to yellow. Dr. Ostwald took the circle further, allowing for greater subtlety with the complementary use of colours. This circle reads: yellow, orange yellow, orange, red orange, red, red violet, violet, blue violet, blue, green blue, green, yellow green.

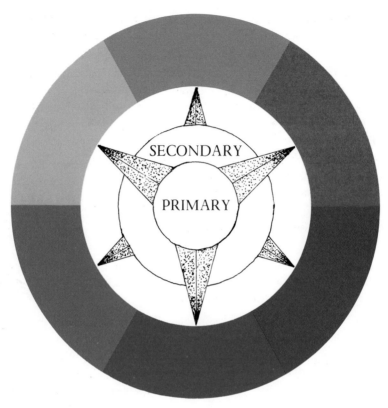

Circle with primary and secondary colours. Opposites give complementaries

Craquelure As an oil painting ages the support may move because of the effects of damp, warmth, and cold draughts. These elements can cause hairline cracks to appear on the face of the picture. The cracks will not necessarily be right through the priming and paint; often they may only be in the varnish.

Diluent A liquid which can be used to dilute or thin down a substance, but not dissolve it.

Driers Substances added to oil colours to speed the drying; the idea is to produce as even a drying time as possible right across the palette.

Dry brush painting A manner for obtaining a broken speckled effect. The brush, generally a flat shape, is given a minimal colour loading. Then, held almost parallel to the picture, it is dragged across the chosen area,

12

leaving light traces of colour – usually just the marks of the individual bristles. It can be exploited for haze, mist, smoke, rain, spray and similar effects.

Drying oils   These include: linseed, poppy, walnut, safflower, hemp seed, sunflower. All these are vegetable oils that dry to a hard leathery film when in thin layers, either alone or with the addition of a metallic salt as a drier. They dry because of a reaction with the oxygen in the air, not from evaporation.

Earths   Pigments which occur naturally in the ground, such as ochre, umber and sienna. Native earths are those which are used raw, e.g. raw umber, raw sienna, yellow ochre. Burnt umber and burnt sienna are calcined earths.

Ebauche   The first underpainting, which should be very low in oil content. It can also be a sketch, a rough draft or an outline.

Fillers   Inert pigments added to more expensive powerful colours which produce lower ranges of colours and are used by schools and students. Kaolin is one of the most used substances.

Frottis   A French term for a thin wash of colour, a glaze; or the veil of colour remaining after any excess has been rubbed away.

Fugitive colours   Pigments that can fade when exposed to strong light or atmospheric pollutants, and also react with other colours in mixtures, darkening and cracking. One of the worst examples is asphaltum (see p. 10).

Grisaille   A monochrome carried out in tones of grey. The result can resemble sculpture or bas-relief. The ancient Greeks used the manner extensively for indicating modelling as they had not the knowledge of chiaroscuro (see p. 47).

Ground   The name that embraces the surface layer on the support which will take the actual painting. Gesso is the ground on many panels (see p. 32). The sizing and priming is the ground on canvas.

Impasto   Heavy application of paint that stands up from the canvas and holds the marks of brushes and painting knives.

Laying-in   The broad application of the underpaint or the first layers of paint.

Lean colour   Paint applied with a low oil content, diluted with turpentine or white spirit.

Marouflage   The process of fixing a canvas to a panel or a wall. The traditional adhesive for this has been white lead and linseed oil. This is spread over the canvas as well as the panel or the wall. The canvas is then laid on the panel or the wall and any wrinkles are eased out with the palms of the hands or a rubber roller. Other adhesives can be wax and resin – laid hot – and water-soluble glues. Care should be taken with many of the modern synthetic adhesives as they can affect the ground layers and the paint.

Medium   There are two meanings here. On the one hand, the medium can imply the method in which the artist works; i.e. oil painting, water-colour, acrylics, etc. On the other hand, it means the liquid or cream additive the painter puts with his oil colours to achieve the working quality he wants.

Oiling out   The rubbing in of a small quantity of a drying-oil to an area of a painting in progress that has sunk and gone flat. Retouching varnish can also be used and is in many ways more satisfactory as it will dry quickly and is less likely to leave any harmful excesses.

Palette   As with the word medium, there is a double meaning. First, it is the object on which the colours are placed and mixed. Secondly, it is the selection of colours from which the painter works.

Pochade   A French word meaning a rough sketch, usually done out of doors direct from nature and intended as a guide for a larger picture.

Stipple   Painting with the brush held more or less at a right angle to the canvas or panel. The paint is put on with short downward strokes leaving small blobs of colour. The manner can be noted by a close look at a pointillist work by Seurat.

Vehicle   The liquid in which the pigments are ground or suspended. Thus, with oil colours the vehicle is an oil; with tempera it is egg-yolk.

Historical development

The mixing of ground pigments with oil was not an instant invention, although for a long time it was attributed to the Flemish painters Jan and Hugo van Eyck. In fact, it was and has continued to be an evolution to answer the needs of artists.

When the process started is impossible to point to with certainty. Pliny makes mention of painting with oils, and that the idea was brought to Italy at the time of Marcellus, and also that the Romans used such paint for decorating their shields. The medical writer Aetius, at the beginning of the sixth century, discusses the use of nut oil. The Lucca Manuscript of the eighth or ninth century gives a recipe for the use of linseed oil and resin. In the Mount Athos Handbook it shows 'peseri' or boiled linseed was in regular use; there is also in this treatise a clear description of the oil-painting technique. A more lucid statement still comes from Theophilus about 1100, who tells the painter to grind his colours carefully in oil of linseed.

What the artists were searching for was a medium that would give them characteristics not found with other earlier methods. By the time of the Van Eycks and the Flemish painters contemporary with them the problems of grinding pigments with oil and resin had to a degree been worked out.

The resulting paint had a number of advantages. The presence of the oil gave a greater richness and brightness to the pigments than when they were used with gum in forms of watercolour, with egg as tempera, or with lime water in fresco. In addition, there was an increase in the flexibility of manipulation, and many more textural and brushing effects became possible. The painter could experiment with the transparency of certain colours, employing glazing and opaque effects. Mistakes could be easily corrected. Further, he would know that there would be little change as his colours dried out.

Any disadvantages that might arise were the results to a large degree of carelessness in the preparation of the paints or in the methods of use, or incorrect preparation of the supports.

It is worthwhile examining cil paintings from the Renaissance, and also those from the early Dutch and Flemish painters. In the majority of these there is a surprisingly high degree of quality of paint surviving, despite attacks from time, moisture, heat, vandalism, and not least the early efforts of restorers.

There are, indeed, cases such as Leonardo's *Virgin of the Rocks*, in the National Gallery, London, where an unwise experiment by the master with the pigments that he used for the plants in the foreground has caused serious deterioration. But, in general, much of the enduring quality of the paint is likely to be the result of skills learnt by artists during their Guild training. Also, because the early painters worked with a very limited palette of colours, they had less opportunity to try unstable pigments.

The oil that has remained the most important for the painter is linseed. Other oils that have been employed with painting include: safflower, as a possible substitute for linseed; the non-yellowing poppy, pressed from the seeds; and walnut from the mature kernels. The last two are inferior to linseed, although in small additions they can be exploited for special cases; for example, poppy will delay drying – an advantage at times with portrait work where the artist has to return to it again and again to fit in with a sitter and yet he feels happier working into wet paint.

Some artists have experimented with such oils as: soya; perilla, which has a strong tendency to yellow; tung, which comes from a nut indigenous to China; oiticica, from Brazil; and lumbang, so called candlenut oil, from the Philippines. There are also sunflower, hempseed, and stillingia, and at least another fifty which have been tried, and which have at times brought disaster to the pictures in which they were used.

There have always been some artists who have been driven on by the desire to obtain elusive or difficult effects. In this pursuit they have used fugitive materials or ill-advised techniques. In the eighteenth century and early nineteenth, many, notably in England, fell for the use of a treacherous pigment, asphaltum or bitumen. Sir Joshua Reynolds, the first President of the Royal Academy, was one who sadly included this vicious colour in his work; but the results of its use can also be noted in pictures by such artists as Hoppner and Wilkie.

Before the advent of the highly skilled artists' colourman, the painter either followed age-proved methods through the Guilds or trusted to the few existing treatises. Today his situation is vastly improved because the spade-work of preparation is done for him, and guesswork as to what is safe has been largely removed.

Artists' colourmen as such had their beginnings in the seventeenth century. The diarist John Evelyn mentions in 1661, in a classified list of trades, a brush-maker and a colour-maker. The products of the latter would probably have been supplied in a pig's bladder to the artist, the neck of the bladder having been most likely knotted round with cord. To use the colours, the painter could pierce the bladder, and having squeezed out the required amount, would plug the hole with a broad-headed tack. Records also show that in the eighteenth century oil colours could be had from shops selling decorators' colours. The problem of the somewhat messy pigs' bladders for holding oil colours was tackled in the first half of the nineteenth century when patent glass syringes were tried. But these were soon eclipsed when in 1841 a collapsible metal tube was invented, and those still used today are basically the same.

Towards the end of the nineteenth century there arose a public outcry voicing opinions that artists were in ignorance of the materials they were using and that many of the colours were fugitive. Makers then started to publish details regarding the composition of their colours. The pigments were classified for permanence, and often listed with foreign translations.

Materials

Choice of colours and speed of drying

Choice of colours

When making a start with oil painting, there is the temptation to buy practically every colour on the charts, and large numbers of other materials that are listed, but oil painting is essentially a technique which must be learnt and mastered by simple steps and an understanding of the materials and the tools involved. Each colour has very definite characteristics, which are affected by brushwork, tonal and tint changes when mixed or when broken with white or when diluted with a painting medium – an oil, turpentine or white spirit. Therefore when a start is made it will be simpler and quicker to become intimate with a short general choice of colours. A point to hold in mind is that it is considerably more economical to buy the largest size tubes available. A starting palette of colours could include the following.

Cadmium yellow Cadmium sulphide. A bright pigment with strong tinting power. It is a comparatively modern colour. It is permanent and has replaced a number of other yellows which were fugitive and had bad habits.

Yellow ochre A native earth containing hydrated ferric oxide. One of the safest and most permanent pigments available to the artist and one which in its natural form has been used since prehistoric times.

Indian red A blend of natural and synthetic oxides of iron. It is permanent and has a subtle blue tinge.

Cadmium red Complex cadmium sulpho-selenides. Has a high degree of permanence and can be had in a number of shades from scarlet to near crimson. It will act as a substitute for the more costly vermilion, and is more stable. It may be less durable in humid conditions.

Alizarin crimson   Prepared from dihydroxyanthraquinone, a derivative of coal tar. Synthetic lakes in this category do not have the delicacy of colour of those obtained from the genuine madder root, but they are more stable, although slow driers.

Viridian   A hydrated and very transparent variety of chromium sesquioxide. A beautiful cool, clear, bright green, quite permanent.

French ultramarine   Complex combinations of silica, alumina, soda and sulphur. It has a similarity to the make-up of genuine ultramarine which is prepared from lapis lazuli, and which it has replaced, mainly for economic reasons.

Burnt umber   Calcined raw umber. A rich powerful colour and quite permanent.

The foregoing eight colours will be found to meet practically every need. But as progress is made and a personal manner is developed, it may also be found that other colours can be successfully included. For instance, with landscape work the following can well play their part.

Naples yellow   A prepared mixture of cadmium yellow, flake white, light red and yellow ochre. It is a pale, cool tint useful with clouds, the bottom areas of skies, reflections on water, and highlight notes for the foreground.

Cobalt blue   Cobalt aluminate or phosphate containing some alumina. Bright, transparent colour with perhaps more subtlety than French ultramarine when broken with white.

Monastral or phthalocyanine blue   Copper phthalocyanine, an organic pigment originally introduced by the Imperial Chemical Industries Ltd in 1937 under the name of 'monastral fast blue'.

Burnt sienna   Calcined raw sienna. A useful strong, warm colour for details and areas of shade with brick buildings, timber palings, fishing boats and suchlike. Broken with white, it has a pleasing range of soft brown-pinks.

Raw umber   A native earth containing ferric oxides and manganese dioxide. Useful for work in cool areas. When broken with white it provides a range of delicate brown-grey tints.

Ivory black   Obtained from the calcination of bones. Originally, as the name suggests, it was made from ivory chips. By itself it can be used with discretion for strong, dark accents. Mixed with cadmium yellow, it will produce a bright, strong range of luscious greens for foliage, field grass or paintwork on buildings. One small note of caution: if it is applied on a smooth white ground, it does have a tendency to crack; but this can largely be obviated by mixing just a touch of some other colour, such as burnt umber, French ultramarine or burnt sienna, with it prior to application.

If the choice is for flower painting, the following colours could be useful.

Lemon yellow   An exceptionally bright, clean colour. Applied pure, it could well simulate, say, sunflower petals or yellow roses; and when mixed with French ultramarine it will produce fresh, sparkling greens.

Permanent magenta   An organic pigment first produced in 1958. A clean, strong colour for picking up the tints of flowers like fuschias and gloxinias. It will be found that mauves and purples are very difficult to mix cleanly, even from such colours as French ultramarine and alizarin crimson. With a specialist colour such as magenta there would be little need to purchase a large tube, a small one would suffice.

Oxide of chromium   Chromium sesquioxide. A beautiful and strong pigment which, broken with white, has a delightful range of cool, sparkling tints; suitable to match up with cacti, cyclamen leaves, stems of daffodils and tulips.

Whatever the selection may be, there must of course be a **white**. To a degree, with oil painting white is similar to water with water colours in that it is used to dilute or break down the stronger colours – hence the term 'broken with white'.

Here the choice rests between flake (basic carbonate of lead with a small percentage of zinc oxide – also known as silver white); titanium (titanium oxide, with a small percentage of zinc oxide – a fine white pigment and a comparatively recent addition to the palette, very dense and opaque, non-poisonous and completely inert); and zinc (oxide of zinc). This last does have a slight tendency to crack and is prone to 'chalking' on some grounds. A number of portrait painters, particularly in the nineteenth century, used it, and this unfortunate characteristic can be noted in some of the faces, especially those of women, as well as in their hands. The cracks at times can be as wide as 3 mm ($\frac{1}{8}$ in) and normally will have to be filled when the painting is restored.

Probably the best of these three when starting to paint is titanium white which has many advantages; it will be found to work well with the brush and will mix readily with the other colours.

Speed of drying

It should be realized that oil colours have appreciable differences in drying times, that is, the time they take to become skin-dry. Overpainting cannot be carried out until the underpainting has become skin-dry. A painting is skin-dry when the paint has formed a dry surface skin, although underneath it may still be soft. Heavy impasto or thick layers of paint may take months, and in certain cases even years, to truly harden right through. With normal painting techniques, quick dryers would take about three to four days to skin-dry, medium about seven days and slow around fourteen days. The palette of colours suggested on pp. 18–20 can be divided up as follows.

Quick dryers	**Medium dryers**	**Slow dryers**
burnt umber	yellow ochre	cadmium yellow
burnt sienna	Indian red	cadmium red
raw umber	oxide of chromium	alizarin crimson
	lemon yellow	French ultramarine
	viridian	ivory black
	Naples yellow	magenta
	monastral blue	
	cobalt blue	
	titanium dioxide	

Alkyd colours, in comparison, all dry at an even speed; and under normal conditions a picture would be 'finger-dry' within eighteen hours and consequently could be overpainted the following day.

Media, diluents and solvents

Having made a choice of colours, it is possible that a medium of some kind will be needed. The colours, as they are supplied in the tubes, will be of sufficient stiffness, or 'short' enough, to stand up when applied with a hog-brush or a painting-knife, but for general work across the canvas some form of diluent should be used. It is important that plenty of time should be spared for 'getting the feel' of the colours by themselves and with additives; this can be carried out on spare pieces of card, canvas paper or similar supports (see p. 23). By doing this it will become apparent how the various media affect the different colours, and just how much of them should be added. Usually, a drop will suffice to increase the fluidity; if too much is added the resulting areas of colour may be thin and starved.

There is a wide choice, and the most suitable for a personal manner can come from one or other of the following.

White spirit   A refined petroleum solvent. Although it will readily thin the colours, the resulting dried film will tend to be matt and rather lowered in power. Inflammable.

Turpentine   Made by distilling the thick resinous sap of pine trees. It will reduce the consistency and improve the flow, and the resulting paint film will not be quite so dull as that left by white spirit. Inflammable.

Media

Linseed oil   In addition to reducing the consistency it will tend to level out brush marks and slow the drying rate.

Poppy oil   Particularly suitable for use with whites and light tints and tones. Slows the drying rate even more than linseed oil and will yellow less.

Copal oil medium   A mixture of linseed oil, gum copal and turpentine. Versions of this were favourites in the nineteenth century. It is a dark yellow liquid that will harden and also darken with age, and if it is used in excess, cracking in depth through the paint film is likely.

Patent painting mediums   Most artists' colourmen market their own proprietary mediums for oil painting. These can contain a variety of ingredients, such as beeswax, turpentine, linseed oil, walnut oil, poppy oil, alkyd resins and other synthetic resins and waxes. These products should be approached with care, and experimented with to find that one which appears to suit the individual style.

In general, beware of thick creamy mediums that can claim to build up extra impasto. Some may be as unreliable as the notorious 'megilp' that was introduced in the eighteenth century, an unpredictable mixture of linseed oil and mastic varnish.

Retouching varnish

During the painting of a picture, if it is carried out over a period of several days or longer, areas of the paint may become 'dried out' and matt and dull, which makes the judging of later work, tonally and tint-wise, very difficult. To remedy this, artists have in the past carried out what is called 'oiling out'. A thin coat of linseed or pure painting medium would be brushed or rubbed over the offending area. This procedure could rectify the optical effect, but it could also leave behind excess oil that could upset the final drying out of a painting and would be likely to encourage cracking or 'rivelling', an unsightly wrinkling of the film.

A far better course is to brush on a thin application of retouching varnish, being careful that it is only put on over areas that are skin-dry. This retouching varnish can be a mixture, such as dammar resin with white spirit, which is a very pale yellow and will dry quickly and restore the gloss to the paint. Retouching varnish may also be used to give an overall temporary protection to a recently completed painting before it is thoroughly dry and ready for the final varnish. Note that it is inflammable, and contact with skin and eyes is to be avoided.

Varnishes

The final varnishing of a picture should not take place until about twelve months have elapsed since it was painted; this is to allow areas of impasto and thick layers to harden.

For this final varnishing, the choice used to be from three natural resin varnishes: copal, the darkest; dammar; and mastic. None of these natural resin varnishes, however, has ever been totally satisfactory. They all tend to darken and yellow with time, to crack because of lack of elasticity and to bloom.

These natural resin varnishes have now been largely superseded by recent synthetic products. They are water clear liquids which will dry quickly under normal conditions and which are non-yellowing and non-blooming, and also they are normally unlikely to crack. Contact with skin and eyes should be avoided, and they are inflammable.

Where it is felt that a matt finish suits a particular painting, there are varnishes available containing either synthetic waxes or beeswax. Generally they will need gentle warming to clarify them before use. They should be applied with a wide brush and as directly as possible. When dry the surface can be lightly buffed with a soft clean rag. There is also a wax paste varnish which is a combination of beeswax and white spirit. This should be sparingly rubbed over the surface of the dried-out picture, left for a few minutes and then gently buffed up with a soft brush or cloth, taking particular care with areas of upstanding or prickly impasto.

Supports

The ground on which a painting is carried out is known as the support. In the long and varied history of oil painting artists have used a wide and at times unwise variety of substances. These have included textiles, woods, metals (generally copper), ceramic plaques, glass (as in back-glass painting), slates, stones, cards, papers and leather.

The three principal supports met with today are: panels (which may be of wood, heavy cardboard, hardboard, canvas board); canvas (generally of pure flax, cotton or, for special purposes where excessive texture is required, sailcloth or hessian); and paper (oil painting paper, rag paper that has been suitably treated).

It is vital that the support should be correctly prepared, see p. 32.

Brushes

The first tools our very distant ancestors used for putting on colours were likely to have been green sticks with ends crushed either by hammering with stones or biting and chewing, or even perhaps small pieces of fur or their fingers. At some time around 2,000 BC the Egyptians produced the early prototype for a painting brush as we know it today. This rather cumbersome object consisted of rush fibre bound to a handle with cord.

Since this innovation there has been much experimentation with materials. Hairs and bristles from a wide variety of animals have been tried:

Types of brush: (*left to right*) flat, white, hog-bristle varnishing brush, round brush, flat brush and filbert

24

pigs, weasels, sables, squirrels, oxen, civets, skunks, badgers, ponies, goats, bears, and even human hair; also baleen fibre from the whale, flight feathers from teal and widgeon, and plant fibres from assorted canes, grasses and palms. More recently, synthetic fibres have been selected with some success.

But for oil painting, time and demand have proved that for the majority of the work hog-bristle is by far the most satisfactory. The principal sources are France, from where comes the firm, silky and very white bristle, and China. Other suppliers include Russia, Poland and some mid-European countries. The process of selection used by the brushmaker is rigorous and only about one-tenth of the bristles obtained from a pig are finally suitable for high quality artists' brushes.

The three best known hog-bristle brushes are the round, the flat and the filbert, which is to a degree a marriage of the first two. Besides these is the 'Herkomer', also termed 'Rubens', which has the bristles set in a flat head but with the curl of them set in towards the centre; it is a shape which gives excellent control, particularly for long sweeping strokes.

At the start, the selection can be kept down to about five. These could be a small and medium size round, small and medium flat and a medium filbert.

Added to the above, there are: riggers, long-hair round sable brushes for detail work; flat sable brushes, where a smooth surface finish is sought; and fans, or sweeteners, intended for delicate and subtle blending or grading. Lastly, a varnish brush will be needed, and here economy can be an error – go for the best. The varnish brush will have to work hard and its quality must be up to the demands; nothing is more troublesome than a poor quality brush that starts shedding bristles half-way through varnishing a painting.

Brushes are very much a craftsman's product; they are made of finest quality materials and will last for a long time if cared for. At the end of a painting session they should never be left clogged with paint. They may be rinsed clean with white spirit. This should be done in a manner so that it does not damage the bristles: stir round and round in a jar of the spirit rather than pound them against the bottom, then draw them through a piece of rag to remove surplus spirit.

Every so often it is wise to give them a thorough washing with warm, not hot, water and plain household soap. Do not use detergents, as these could affect and deteriorate the settings. The best way is, having moistened the brushes, to gently rub them on to a piece of good quality plain soap and then brush them around in the palm of the hand, and repeat the process until all colour has come away. Next, rinse out well in cold water and gently ease the bristles or hairs back into their correct set. Finally, leave the brushes to dry out, standing upright in a jar or a can. If they are to be stored away for a long period, it is best once they are dry to lay them in a drawer or a box that has a slight tilt in the base. As moth larvae have a predilection for bristles and hairs, one of the moth-discouraging substances can be put with them.

Knives

From the start it is convenient to have a palette-knife, as it will greatly facilitate the cleaning of the palette. The blade should be straight and have a fair degree of flexibility, and when it is pressed down it should lie flat. It is best to use the proper article for cleaning wooden palettes, as an ordinary knife with its sharp, firm edge can very soon damage the wood. The palette-knife can also be used for mixing paint if desired.

The difference between palette-knives and painting knives is that the latter have cranked handles; the principal reason for this being that the fingers holding the handle are kept clear of the paint when working. Therefore it is wise when buying these knives to make sure the crank is sufficient to allow this to happen. The shapes of the blades vary from quite small trowels to elongated ones similar to palette-knives. It is essential that the blades of painting knives should be very flexible so as to allow for sensitivity and control when working.

Palettes

There are three shapes to choose from: the oblong, the hook or oval, and the kidney, balanced or studio. The oblong is in some ways the most convenient for outside work because it will generally fit into the oil paintbox. Palettes are made in mahogany, mahogany plywood, birch plywood and various plastics. When the palette is new it will be easier to work with the colours if, before use, it is given a good 'oiling up' with linseed, rubbing the oil well in and leaving it to soak for two or three days. After that time any excess can be wiped away with a rag dipped in white spirit.

For outside work especially, an expendable palette can be serviceable. This consists of a pad of fifty or so vegetable parchment sheets that have been treated so as to be impervious to oil. At the end of a day's work the top sheet with the paint residues can be torn off and disposed of, so avoiding a lot of cleaning up.

For studio work, if one has a painting table, a sheet of plate glass can be cut to fit the top, and if a sheet of cartridge paper is laid underneath the glass, a very serviceable palette will result.

Dippers

The purchase of a dipper can save trouble when painting. This little gadget is intended to hold the medium or oil being used and it clips on to the side of the palette. If possible, get one with a screw or hinged lid, because this will prevent the medium or oil drying out too quickly.

Mahl stick

A long thin cane or bamboo which has a soft pad on one end. It is held with the pad against the canvas to provide a steadying rest for the brush hand when fine detail work and particular accents are being executed.

Canvas pins

It is well worth while buying a box of these, as they make the carrying of two wet canvases easier. They consist quite simply of small plastic or wood

blocks with double steel points. Fix one in each corner of a wet canvas and then push the second canvas on to the exposed points. The whole can be secured with a strap or a piece of cord.

Easels

The choice is varied and can depend on individual needs and finance. The most important things to look for, at whatever price, are: (a) that there is good stability; (b) that it is simple to fix the canvas or panel and that this will be held firmly; (c) that it is possible to give a tilt to the canvas – an essential point when painting out-of-doors so as to allow for better sighting, particularly when the sun is overhead or at an awkward angle.

Light sketching easels are made either of hardwood or aluminium, but it should be borne in mind that these types will not hold canvases much above 609 × 508 mm (24 × 20 in) with comfort. In windy weather extra stability can be given by suspending a heavy stone by a cord from the juncture of the three legs.

It is well worth the necessary extra expenditure for a slightly heavier sketching easel. This can be constructed from beechwood and should be adjustable. When fully extended it should carry a canvas up to 1270 mm (50 in) high, either upright or tilted forward to any desired angle. Further, by moving the vertical arm to a more horizontal position it can also be used for watercolour sketching.

For professional work, a full studio easel is undoubtedly the most satisfactory. This should be of heavy construction and should take a canvas of at least 1827 mm (72 in); there are some monsters that will comfortably and firmly hold a canvas up to 3046 mm (120 in). They will generally be raised, lowered and tilted by crank handles working on long grub screws. Sadly for painters, such fine pieces of craftsmanship are more and more becoming collectors' items and if bid for in a saleroom are liable to fetch several hundred pounds or dollars.

The studio

These days the number of artists who can hope to have a custom-built studio must be small. But a compromise can often be remarkably effective. There have been cases where a leading portrait painter manages quite comfortably in a small garden-shed, or an abstract artist works away in a bedroom, or a marine painter adapts a fisherman's loft in a West-Country port.

If possible, a room should be set aside which will only be used for painting. For a professional this is essential, and even for a beginner it is a luxury which will soon be compensated for by the outright enjoyment that will be experienced when a studio atmosphere is created.

Daylight

Lighting is the single most important feature. Where possible, aim to have the main window or skylight facing north in Britain and the northern hemisphere (south in the southern hemisphere). The reason is that this aspect will provide the most constant source of light and will not admit direct sun's rays. If this is not possible, north-east or east is next best in the northern hemisphere.

Where there is no alternative to directly facing the sun, some help can be had from muslin or net curtains, or even venetian blinds where the slats are made of milky white plastic. Should the chosen studio be unfortunately sited low down in a building which is set rather close to its neighbour, extra light can be brought in by arranging a large slanted mirror outside the window.

Artificial light

This can be a rather vexed question where painting is concerned, because some colours, notably French ultramarine, appear considerably darker under it. Normally, tungsten electric light bulbs will not provide a satisfactory light source because, apart from their effects on colours, they are difficult to position so that they project an even light on the easel and on the subject. It is better to invest in either a simple, long warm-white fluorescent tube or a bank of several short tubes of this type. The simple long tube can be fixed directly over the top of the window or right under the bottom of the skylight in order to approximate the position of the natural light source. If a bank of short tubes is chosen, they should be mounted in a head on a stand which will allow them to be moved to suit any particular need.

Walls and ceiling

A feature often overlooked is the decoration of the studio. Gaudy, over-bright wallpaper or paint scheme will not only catch and disturb the eye, but will create unwelcome reflections. The best plan is to distemper or emulsion paint the walls a pale, neutral, slightly warm grey. It may be possible to find this ready-mixed at a decorators' supplier. If not, it is quite a simple matter to mix a suitable tint. To white distemper or emulsion, add small quantities of French ultramarine, yellow ochre and light red in powder colour form. The ceiling should be left white.

Floors

Some form of protective floor-covering is useful. A good cork linoleum will generally stand up to spillages of white spirit, oils and varnishes. Some of the plastic-based coverings will not, nor will some of the synthetic floor tiles and rubber tiles; these are all liable to dissolve or become spongy and tacky.

Heating

Here the main thing to remember is that a number of the materials being used will be inflammable; therefore the source chosen should not, if possible, have exposed elements or flames. A storage heater can be excellent, as can an oil-filled electric radiator.

Painting table

One other item that is well worth considering from the start is a painting table. Whether it is used with a plate-glass top (see p. 26) is a matter of choice. If you can find an old table with some drawers in a sale, all the better. If not, adapt one or have it done for you so that there may be a provision for storing tubes, bottles of oils, media and varnish, as well as places for the correct storage of brushes. The table should be mounted on large castors or small swivelling wheels for ease of movement.

Procedures and techniques

Oil painting has in many ways given considerable freedom to the artist: the chance to use a variety of brush strokes and textures, intensity of colour on one hand, subtlety on the other, and a brightness and richness not provided by any other type of paint. All of these can be exploited with safety and the results will be permanent if a few basic disciplines are observed.

The examination of oil paintings in galleries, particularly those produced in the last two hundred years, can be instructive. The effects of colours such as asphaltum or zinc white have already been remarked on, and there are other impermanences and disfigurements that can be noted; for instance, undue cracking, 'rivelling' of the paint film, as well as flaking from lack of adhesion or the ground giving way. Even with the work of artists of this century there are pictures which already need the attention of a restorer, although they may have been painted only about ten years ago.

The reasons for this are in most cases simple. The painter has quite plainly disregarded the basic tenets of his craft. This may be from ignorance or insufficient care with materials, or because of too much haste. But whatever the cause, there is really no excuse. A number of modern paintings are in a bad condition because the artist incorporates additives which are just not suited to the medium if the picture is to survive the years.

It is absolutely essential for permanence that the support is correctly sized and/or primed, and that it is thoroughly dried out before painting begins. Then, the basic rule of the house-painter should be followed, which is to start lean and finish fat. This means that the final layers of paint should be richer in oil than the underpainting so that the danger of cracking or flaking may be avoided. If these rulings are kept to, one is well on the way to achieving lasting qualities.

Never mix such substances as kaolin, marble dust, whiting, sand, sawdust or cement into the paint in the hope of building up more robust and powerful impasto and textures. With oil painting such practices are likely to cause disaster.

Preparation of supports

Many of the troubles that have afflicted oil paintings stem from the fact that the supports have not been prepared correctly. It is important that they should be non-absorbent, and this should be effected by thorough isolation, which is normally done by brushing over with size or shellac before the priming is applied. The support should also have an adequate 'key' for the paint, that is, it should have a slightly rough surface for the paint to grip.

If the isolation is inadequate the richness of the oil colours will be diminished, as the oils soak into the support rather than dry out to the surface so as to maintain their strength, depth and warmth. Further, if textiles are not isolated or sized, the oil can cause the fibres to rot prematurely.

Panels

Many of the early masters painted on wooden panels and they took great pains to see that all the preparation work was thorough. Woods that have been used include poplar, pine, oak, beech and mahogany. After the wood had been well seasoned it would be grounded with gesso – a term which broadly means a mixture of plaster and glue, the favourite glue being that made from rabbit skin, because it is almost colourless and a hard setter.

The laying of the gesso on to the selected panel was a long process. Often a piece of muslin or thin linen would be sized down first and then the gesso put on in several layers, the first of which would be fairly coarse and was called *gesso grosso*. This process led up to the final *gesso sottile* which was quite liquid and carefully strained to leave behind a perfect surface. After the panel had set for a month or more the gesso would have hardened and when rubbed down would come up with an ivory-like appearance and feel.

If the painter was one such as the early German Stefan Lochner (active 1442–51), the panel would be further prepared, as he like others of his time employed gold leaf for part of the picture. First, a thin coat of red earth, Armenian bole, mixed with size would be applied. When that had hardened the adhesive for the gold leaf would be brushed on. This was often 'glair', a mixture of well-beaten egg-white and water. Then the wafer-thin leaf would be lowered into place using a wide flat brush called a 'tip'. Apart from the use of ornamental stamps pressed into the leaf, it was intended that the artist should use transparent colours over the leaf, so that the sheen of the gold would come through and increase their luminosity.

If preparing a panel in a somewhat simpler vein, pieces of hardboard or heavy card may be used. Heavy card should hold its shape up to 254 × 305 mm (10 × 12 in) and hardboard up to 406.4 × 508 mm (16 × 20 in); if these sizes are exceeded, it is wise to put a frame support round the edges of the backs of the panels to prevent warping. When using hardboard it is better to paint on the smooth side, because the rough has a reverse negative impression of canvas which is not happy to work on, also it will take up a lot of colour.

The painting surfaces of hardboard or heavy card can be treated either with size and an oil painting primer or by coating with an acrylic primer. When using the latter, if the surface of the panel is hard and non-absorbent, it may be found that one coat is sufficient; but if the primer sinks, a first coat can be given which has been slightly diluted with water and this followed later by a second. The acrylic primer gives a flexible coating with good adhesion, provided the underlying support is non-oily. It will dry to a white matt surface with sufficient 'tooth' to ensure satisfactory adhesion for the paint layer. Oil primed boards should not be used for acrylic painting.

If a glue size is used, it should be prepared in a double saucepan or glue-pot, care being taken not to exceed the strength suggested with the instructions. The sized panel should be left overnight to dry out and then the oil painting primer may be brushed on.

Canvases

For many people, when painting in oils the most pleasing support is canvas. There is something about the feel, the elasticity to the brush, and the texture of the various weaves found only with a canvas stretched on a wooden frame. The slight natural tooth of canvas lends itself more to the oil technique than does the polished smooth surface of gesso which calls for a more deliberate and planned manner.

If preparing a canvas, the choice can be from a number of surfaces, fine weave to coarse, and also, as mentioned, materials such as sailcloth and hessian may be used. Synthetic textiles are not suitable. The important point is that whatever is chosen, it must be prepared correctly; either of the methods described for hardboard (above) will suffice. If correct sizing and priming are not carried out, the longevity of the painting will be seriously threatened.

When putting the canvas on to the stretcher, watch that the frame is absolutely square. This can be done by measuring the diagonals with a piece of string, or shaping the stretcher up against the corner of a table-top.

Putting the canvas on a stretcher. (*above*) When cutting canvas to shape leave sufficient to fold over on to the back of the stretcher. (*below*) Use straining pliers to hold canvas tight when tacking on to stretcher

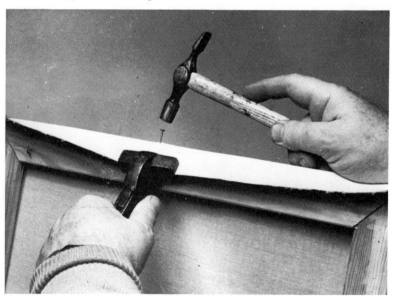

Further, align the warp and weft of the canvas so that they run parallel with the sides of the frame. Next, raise the stretcher and canvas on edge and place the first tack or staple in the centre of the top side; turn the support over and place the next tack or staple opposite the first, having applied a pull with the straining pliers. Repeat the operation in the centres of the other two sides. Now, work towards one corner at a time, fixing first on one side, then the next; care being taken all the time to get an even stretch to the canvas.

Ready-primed canvas either in rolls or on standard size stretchers can save much time and the choice is various, textures and weaves ranging from fine to coarse.

Papers

Some painters have used different papers for small-scale oil sketches, Holbein was one, and these works have survived reasonably well. But it should be pointed out that the earlier papers would have been made from good-quality rags and not from wood-pulp.

If paper is to be used, it is best that it should be first mounted on a stiff card. It should then be prepared first with either an acrylic primer or size and then the oil painting primer. Any of the rag-papers will answer but it is better to avoid wood-pulp, for even if sized and primed, this does not really answer as a permanent support, and the sketch which comes off successfully could be in jeopardy.

Ready-prepared oil-sketching papers can be bought in sizes up to 762 × 508 mm (30 × 20 in). It is wise always to mount these on hardboard or cardboard, either by sticking them down completely or by temporarily holding them in place with adhesive tape, to avoid curling.

Setting out the palette

This may sound elementary, but the intention behind it is that, when painting, all the procedure taking place apart from the actual painting should be as simple and as comfortable for the artist as possible.

If one grows into the habit of using a recognized order of colours on the palette, it will save time when mixing, as the brush will be more likely to go automatically to the right place.

With the colours suggested on pp. 18 and 19, a good pattern for arrangement round the palette would be, starting from the left: burnt umber, viridian, French ultramarine, alizarin crimson, Indian red, cadmium red, yellow ochre, cadmium yellow, titanium white. Put the colours near to the edge of the palette to leave as much room as possible for mixing.

Studio palette with paints

The palette should balance comfortably on the thumb when loaded, and if the chamfering round the thumb is not quite right, this can generally be remedied by the use of some sandpaper. In action the palette will be supported by lying along the forearm.

As to how much of each colour should be squeezed out when beginning to work, there is no real way to measure this other than by experience. There is also no way to stop the colours drying on the palette if a subject is being worked on for a number of days. Some people have suggested that excess colour at the end of a day can be lifted off with a palette-knife and put on a piece of glass which should then be submerged in water; but this is not advisable, as, apart from the messy part of the procedure, water should be kept well away from the paint film. If some of the quick-drying colours should skin over after a few days, the skin can be carefully removed with the palette-knife before restarting painting.

At the completion of a subject it is wise to clean off the palette. First, lift and scrape off what excess paint you can with the palette-knife, holding it so that it does not damage the wood. Any paint that has hardened can be softened and cleared away by using a paint solvent or remover. Such a liquid can be used safely for cleaning brushes when hardened paint has been allowed to accumulate, and also for hard dried paint on the palette. Care should be taken to protect the eyes from the solvent or remover. Breathing too much of the vapour should be avoided and adequate ventilation in the room is desirable – smoking while using these fluids is not advisable. After wiping off the softened paint, rinse the brushes and the palette with white spirit to take away all traces of the remover. Lastly, wipe a rag with a few drops of linseed oil over the areas of the palette where the remover has been applied.

Imprimatura

Although numerous painters have been attracted by the staring white rectangle of a virgin primed canvas, others have felt it helpful before they started working to apply a thin wash of colour over the whole surface and this is called imprimatura. This course can be a good practice because the problem of having to 'kill' all the white as one works is removed. Furthermore, an undercolour can form part of the finished picture. John Constable in many of his paintings used to apply a warm earth imprimatura before he began and then deliberately leave areas of this showing through, particularly amongst the shadows, round the boles of trees and in similar places.

A warm burnt sienna with some burnt umber makes an excellent imprimatura where there are large areas of grass, such as with sunlit meadows. Small flecks of this undertone showing through give a luscious feeling to the turf; the eye receives both colours, but the brain interprets the effect as a brighter green, in accordance with the complementary colour theory (see Colour circle, p. 12). Those tints on the opposite sides of the colour circle react most strongly to each other. If an imprimatura is to be laid, it is imperative that it should be thoroughly lean and thin. Sufficient white spirit should be mixed with variable amounts of yellow ochre, burnt sienna, raw and burnt umber to suit personal needs and to produce a consistency which can be washed over the canvas or panel. The support should be ready for painting after about two hours, depending on the evaporation rate of the white spirit.

If desired, the imprimatura can be laid using alkyd colours and white spirit, or true egg tempera, or acrylic colours well diluted with water.

You can save time by treating a whole batch of canvases and panels together when you have the liquid colour mixed up.

Although a warm earth imprimatura has been mentioned, painters have used other colours according to the results they wanted to achieve with their subjects, for instance, cool greens, close to terre verte, for figure painting or blues and darker greens for marine work. Other variations can be arrived at by trying out the proposed top colour over them.

Colour mixing

The secret or trick for successfully mixing two or more colours together is that it should be done as directly as possible, with as little puddling about with a brush as will suffice to bring up the desired tint. The more stroking and rubbing around with a brush that is done in a mix on the palette, the more the resulting colour will 'come down' in brightness and sparkle, and the more likely it is to resemble dull, unpleasant mud.

As much practice as possible should be done on odd scraps of card or paper to achieve the directness and boldness that is necessary to produce a striking and successful tint from a mix. Even with the limited palette of colours indicated on pp. 18–19, there are almost infinite possibilities of mixes.

Work away with unlikely combinations and it is possible that unsuspected riches for future use will emerge. Indian red with viridian and much titanium white can make subtle greys; burnt umber, French ultramarine and cadmium yellow can create deep soft greens. Burnt sienna and cadmium yellow can produce a fiery deep orange. The variations are almost endless. By exercises in mixing colours an intimate knowledge about colour behaviours will be absorbed, so that, when painting, the choice of pigments for a particular passage, highlight or shadow area will come to mind almost automatically.

In many cases the colours coming direct from the tubes will be of the right consistency for what is required, but if it is felt that greater fluidity is needed, add just a few drops of one of the oils or media mentioned on p. 22. Be careful, however, that this addition is kept to the minimum, because if the resulting dilution is too great, the colour will dribble down the canvas, and also the paint will not hold the marks of the bristles of the brush. Oil painting is very much a method of texture; each painter has his own handwriting in the strokes he makes, but these will only ring out if the paint is 'short' (stiff) enough to retain the brush marks.

How important this textural 'handwriting' is in oil painting can be understood if works by some of the masters are examined closely and if at the same time it can be imagined what the pictures might look like, should this textural appearance be missing and all the paint be just flat.

Study some of the works by Frans Hals; see how the hands, the features are indicated by broad bravura strokes. Examine the impassioned pecking stabs of colour in a Van Gogh, the long sweeping motion-filled strokes by Rubens, the rough texture of Rembrandt's highlights on flesh and his immeasurably deep rich shadows, the broken colour used with the restless brush strokes of Pissarro and Sisley. Look at the strange stippling of Seurat, where the artist is attempting to make the viewer's eye do most of the work – for a green, many tiny specks of yellow would be interspersed with specks of blue so that the mind behind the eye would report that it had received a vision of green.

Brushwork

When trying out the possibilities with the mixing of the colours on the palette, experiment also with the three main brush shapes in your box. Each of these is capable of a lot more than a simple downstroke. Held in different ways they will achieve a wealth of varying brushmarks. Try, for example, holding each brush with the handle lying down across the palm, holding it so that it is almost vertical with the bristles pointing down, holding it nearly flat to the canvas, or straight down at a right angle for stippling. The grip should be adaptable for free invention; don't feel there are laws which will constrict you in such matters. Technique has often been confused with an iron discipline emanating from some dusty directory, but it is better thought of as an understanding of what the colours, brushes, knives and general materials will do. In fact, technique should be the key to a freedom which brings in its wake the great enjoyment of painting.

Besides exploring the working quality of the brushes, investigate the possibilities of a single stroke or a series of similar strokes, drawing or colouring a small detail in one action; for example, a flat loaded brush can do this when held in the correct manner for a block or a brick wall. Held so that it presents the blade of its head to touch the canvas, it can produce

Holding the brush in the usual pencil grip

Holding the brush underhand can give a range of different strokes

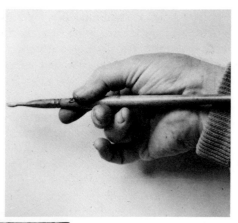

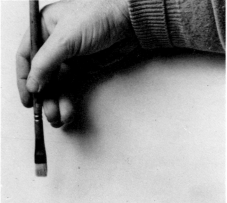

Holding the brush nearly flat and parallel to the canvas for dragging strokes

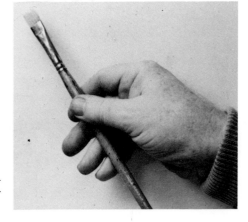

Holding the brush lightly between fingers and thumb for gentle sensitive strokes

representations of rushes, reeds or long grass. Almost dry and dragged across the canvas, it will give a broken effect, such as might be seen on an old flaking plastered wall. The round brush stippled down can build up the soft woolliness of white clouds. Twirling it in the fingers during a stroke can create the likeness of the ripples caused by a soft breeze across a calm sea. The short stabbing strokes of a filbert (p. 24) can give a resemblance to stubble in a harvested cornfield, and well-loaded with slightly diluted colour this brush can produce undulating strokes of great length, as might be needed when portraying the waters of a swollen stream.

The rigger (p. 25), with its brush-head of sable or ox-hair, will nearly always require the colour to be quite substantially diluted. This can be with an oil or a specialist medium, or with white spirit which allows for a very fine mark. The best way of using the rigger is to hold it at about a 45-degree angle along the direction of travel; in this way it will be found that the stroke will have a greater accuracy. If it is held differently, the long head of hair with its delicate point can wander.

On your painting table or close to your easel, it is essential to have a jar of white spirit in which the brushes can be swirled and cleaned when changing to a different colour.

One further point, with the use of the brush and also the knife, do all the mixing on the palette, never on the canvas or panel. The latter course will only lead to mess and mud.

Brush stroke textures

End of Day, Van Gogh
(*Christie's*). This clearly
shows his short, sharp
strokes

Knife painting

An exciting and stimulating action, but one which is probably best left until the groundwork with the brush is well understood. For, to succeed, the artist must be sure enough to apply his colours with directness so that they are right first time down, just as in fresco.

One of the principal differences between brush and knife painting is that, whereas the brush leaves a ribbed textural mark, the sweep of the knife blade tends to leave behind a series of flat surfaces.

For working with a knife, unless incomparably assured, a fairly firm drawing is best prepared on which the strokes can be placed.

More paint will be needed than for brush painting, but it is important that some control is exercised. The thickness of paint must not be allowed to exceed 3 mm ($\frac{1}{8}$ in), or for ridges and very small upstanding areas 5 mm ($\frac{3}{16}$ in). It is simply no good, when working in oils, to go on piling up the

Roses (detail) by the author (*Private Collection*). Knife painting on burnt umber imprimatura with final glaze of raw umber

43

Painting knife strokes

colour. This will not be permanent and will crack and tend to slide and dribble down the canvas.

As with brushes, different methods of holding the knives will produce a variety of marks. The edge, the point, the belly of the blade, all have parts to play. Patting downwards lifts a prickly texture. Loading one side of the knife with one colour and the other side with a second can result, if judged carefully, in a very lively passage – perhaps across a stormy sky, a flooding river or the flames from a bonfire.

Drawing in

Many of the teachers of the nineteenth century would have advocated the closest attention to detail and accuracy when laying in the drawing on a canvas or panel. Although the main skeleton of the drawing should be correct, it is possible that too much attention to the minutiae at the early stage can constrict and take the initial excitement out of painting.

If a sense of freedom is lost, areas of the picture, or even the whole of it, may manifest a feeling of tightness, meanness. This can be avoided by going straight in with the small round brush using a mixture of burnt umber and

Keep drawing in with a brush very simple, and do it with weak diluted colour

French ultramarine well diluted, to almost water-like consistency, with white spirit.

Size up your subject. Half-close the eyes. Simplify it down to the main masses, and then quite broadly indicate these important lines, planes and objects. Don't get caught up at this stage with the number of palings in a fence, individual branches on a tree, how many petals there are round the

45

face of a sunflower, the engraving on a copper pot, or the rigging of yachts at their moorings.

Get the initial 'bones' well balanced and in the right place, and then your foundation for the whole is assured. If you do find that some of these first lines are incorrect, it is a simple matter to dip a paint-rag into the jar of white spirit and wipe out the error; then just give the area a few minutes to dry before making the correction.

Should you feel a little unsure about going straight in with the brush, the same broad preliminary outline strokes could be put in with either a soft pencil or charcoal. These drawings should then be stabilized with a fixative, applied either from a pressurized can or by using a spray diffuser orally. Hold the applicator about 25 cm (10 in) away from the canvas, which should be laid flat, and give two or three light bursts of spray. Be careful not to flood the canvas, or your drawing will float away.

Composition

With the initial drawing in, consideration should be given to composition, which is one of the key factors in picture making. It is the harmonious arrangement of the components of a painting so that they are in happy relationship to one another, and also contained successfully within the rectangle of the canvas or panel. Some artists have worked out various rules on mathematical grounds, using geometry and other sciences, yet really it is a matter which relies mostly on the painters sensitivity, his 'feel' for what is right.

There are a number of basic points, however, that might be suggested. To a degree, symmetry is best avoided and asymmetry used. The latter seems to pull the viewer's eye into a painting more successfully, although straightaway it must be conceded that there are pictures, such as the famous *The Avenue at Middelharnis* (in the National Gallery, London), by the Dutch painter Meindert Hobbema (1638–1709), in which there is an almost perfectly symmetrical avenue of trees right in the centre of the picture.

It is probably better to avoid placing the horizon line in a landscape exactly in the middle of the canvas, as it may give the impression that the composition has been divided in two. Likewise, with a still life or a flower-piece it is unwise to place a feature too directly in the centre.

With any subject, care needs to be exercised as to how a main feature which extends beyond the edge of a canvas is treated. Too often one sees a painting that gives the impression of having been cut down; this may be

46

because the artist has either unwisely omitted a part of the composition or added a superfluous form to one side.

Care is also needed that the centre group of forms in a landscape, a still life or a flower-piece is not made too small or insignificant, otherwise the appearance will be that they are lost in too large a canvas. Opposed to this, the main forms should not be over-drawn, that is, put in so large that they appear to crowd the picture and again suggest it has been cut down.

Some find it helpful to use a piece of card with a central rectangle cut out as a viewfinder. This can be held up at varying distances from the eye and moved over the scene to help in assessing just where it is best to pick the composition from. Similarly, a reducing glass can also give some assistance with the choosing of the subject of a picture.

Light

The general arrangement of light and shade should be worked out and indicated at an early stage, for areas of shade in particular can often unbalance the whole composition if put in later and not well placed. In observing shadows, look well to note how much detail can be seen in them. Shadows put in as just dark masses will appear untrue and take the life out of a picture. Rembrandt was one of the supreme masters of light and shade. His *The Adoration of the Shepherds* (in the National Gallery, London) is an example of the handling of shade, with so much going on in the shadows, the subtle detailing of the rafters of the old stable and the figures standing to the right; the colours are dark and warm, not cold.

The theory and treatment of light and shade are often referred to as 'chiaroscuro'. This is the study and observation of a colour in light and the same colour when in shade. In many ways the training of the eye to pick out the truth of this matter from what it sees is one of the hardest things to attain. As well as in the work of Rembrandt, excellent examples of the use of light and shade can be found in the pictures of such painters as Titian, Caravaggio, Joseph Wright of Derby, Chardin, Fantin-Latour, whose soft subtleties of shade and modelling bring a marvellous quality to flowers, and Monet, particularly with his handling of the deceptive shadows in the snow scenes at Vétheuil.

Pentimento

It is wise to bear in mind a certain odd feature which can occur with an oil painting; this is the ghosting through of an underpainting and it is called *pentimento*. The most usual cause is that an artist has had a change of mind

Self Portrait, Rembrandt (*Christie's*). Note the soft subtle handling of modelling and control of light and shade and a light-toned passage has been painted over an earlier version which may incorporate some dark areas. The main reason for this ghostlike appearance is a change in the refractive index in the vehicle in which the pigments are ground. These *pentimenti* can sometimes be quite disfiguring; in the National Gallery, London, there is an *Interior of a Dutch House* by Pieter de Hooch where the tessellated flooring can be seen clearly through the maidservant's skirt. To guard against such defects, any errors or passages where alterations are desired in drawing or underpainting should be completely removed before overpainting. One strange fact is that photography will very often reveal the presence of *pentimenti* before they become visible to the human eye.

Underpainting

There are two ways in which an oil painting can be carried out after the initial drawing is completed; in two layers, under and overpainting, or the direct single layer method called *alla prima* (see p. 51). The underpainting or *abbozzo* can be worked either as a monochrome or in colours low in tone leading up to the intended final coats. The purpose of the laying in of an undercoat is that it helps considerably to judge aesthetically the progress and the intent of the painting. It should not in any way challenge in brilliance the final colours. If laid with oil paints, the undercoat should be lean, the colours being diluted with white spirit and allowed to dry out thoroughly before the later layers are applied.

Experiments can be undertaken to discover the effect of employing tints for underpainting which are complementary to the final colours that will eventually cover them. For example, artists have used warm red-browns for underpainting grass which gives a particularly luscious look to the fresh greens. The principle here is similar to that described for imprimatura on p. 37. For an explanation of complementary colours, see Colour circle, pp. 11 and 12.

There is a danger, however, that if the early coat is too strong, the brightness of the final colour may be dulled. In general, underpainting is best kept as cool as possible.

For flesh painting, Uccello (c. 1397–1475) used a green underpaint, in contrast to Leonardo (1452–1519) who employed purple. Crome (1768–1821) liked a warm reddish tone for the foundation of skies and raw sienna for foliage and foreground. As with many aspects of painting, in whatever medium, it can become confusing as one gives more study to the ways of the masters, because each individual seems to work out his own particular approach.

The one constant to remember is that the underpaint must be lean, and must be allowed ample time to dry. Any attempt to work into it whilst it is still soft will almost inevitably bring a poor result; the colours will muddy together and freshness will be lost.

If desired, the alkyd colours can be used for underpainting, although when diluted in a similar manner to oils for this purpose there will be no great gain; they may work with a slight increase in fluidity, but their especial attractive qualities are more suitable for later layers with impasto or glazing, see pp. 51 and 54.

Yet another method of underpainting is tempera, which was much in favour with early masters and in which the pigments are mixed with egg-yolk and then diluted with water. The tempera film provides a very stable foundation for oil colours on most supports. Egg tempera will dry out quickly and afterwards there will be no further movement of the film. Corrections are simple to make in the first few minutes of application; a damp sponge or rag will soon wash away what is not wanted.

Attempts have been made, when working on gesso, paper or card, to use watercolour as a base for oils. It is not very satisfactory, but if tried it should be given a thin coat of varnish before working in with the oils. Acrylics may also be used, but in this case it is important that they should be well diluted, nearly to wash consistency.

Overpainting

As mentioned on p. 39, one of the great beauties of oil painting lies in the rich variety of effects produced by different textures and brush strokes. If these qualities are to be achieved in the final layer, it is important that the colours should be kept 'short' enough to preserve the marks of the brushes. If too great an amount of a medium is added the liveliness and the crispness will be lost. It is from trial and experience in general that one can best ascertain how much diluent to mix in to suit a personal manner.

Try to be as direct as possible. Don't fall for the lure of putting down an unthought-out brush stroke and then feel, if it is not quite right, that the colour can be pushed around on the canvas. It can, of course, but the result will stick out as a 'poor' area. Time spent in looking at a subject intently and comparing it closely with the painting in progress is an investment. Decide just where a stroke is going before it lands.

Clean the brushes in between colour mixes, rinsing several times in white spirit and drying with a rag, and this, with the sparing use of the medium already emphasised, will capture an effect of freshness and brightness. Don't get hooked on a particular brush stroke because it appears effective; it may be excellent for the original purpose, but if it is repeated over large areas monotony will soon set in.

Alla prima

This is the making of a painting in one sitting or session. It was regarded by the older schools as the peak as craftsmanship. The artist must have, to a high degree, a fully developed plan for the picture in his mind before he starts to paint. No underpainting is made, other than perhaps the laying of an imprimatura. From the start the aim must be to achieve the final effect in the shortest and most direct manner. Modelling, light and shade, and colour must all be observed at the same time. The virtue of this approach is that an immediate freshness is obtained which cannot quite be captured by the method of underpainting and overpainting just described. Directness is even more important, for even a small correction may mar the finished result.

Work from the beginning for the total effect. Beware of becoming too much involved with an individual area and bringing this to completion while the rest of the canvas stays blank. Stand well back with the brush held long, and attempt to bring the whole along together, sensing balance and colour harmony. As far as possible leave the deepest shadows and the most sparkling highlights until the end.

As the completion of a direct painting is approached, it will be best to look and consider well just where these last strokes should go. Often the final 'lift' may be only a matter of one or two flicks which will bring the whole together and pulse life into the subject. Better to stop a little sooner than to go on too long and overwork so that the life is lost, and the dullness of over-reliance on technique takes over.

Impasto

A general term for the ridges and marks made in the applied colours by brushes and knives – the opposite of when the paint film is reduced to a flat, smooth surface by soft-hair brushes.

It is the very life and attraction of oils for many people. Normally, as the paints come from the tubes they will be found stiff enough to hold the impasto. It is best to use them in this way, as the addition of more oil or a medium will soften them and tend to blur the marks.

The thing to avoid is being carried away by the delicious experience of working with large amounts of thick, rich, colour. By its nature oil paint, where the pigment is mixed with an oil for a vehicle, will not dry out safely if the colours are applied too thickly. An exact maximum thickness cannot be given, because various factors, such as the particular pigment, support and oil, can cause variations. But, if 5 mm ($\frac{3}{16}$ in) thick is taken as an upper limit, the picture should dry out safely.

Sgraffito

A method by which the colour can be manipulated once it is on the support. It means literally cutting into the wet paint, either with a pointed instrument, such as a brush handle-end, or with a scraper tool. If desired, the manner can be carried quite far. Areas can be scraped with combs or specially cut pieces of card. The underpainting can be tinted with sgraffito in mind. For example, a bright yellow first layer can be laid and then overpainted with a strong burnt umber, so that a powerful effect is obtained when the top layer is scratched or scraped through.

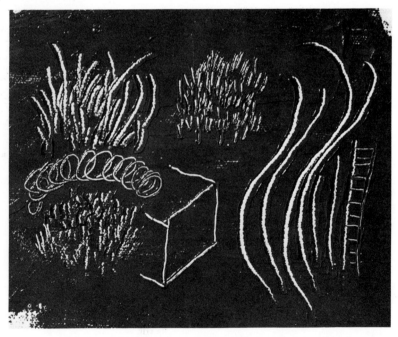

Sgraffito into wet paint with a painting knife and brush handle point

Still Life with Fishing Net, Picasso (*Sotheby's*). This is a good example of sgraffito, cutting through the paint layers to expose the white priming

Glazing

The secret of some of the most luminous passages in a great painting often lies in the glazing. In its simplest form this consists of applying a wash-like film of colour over a previously painted and dried-out area. The result is enrichment and a sense of translucence not present before. Usually, the procedure is to pass a glaze of a dark colour over a light tone which has already been put on. But this need not be a rigid rule – experiment can be made reversing the process and the effect can be a sheen on dark browns, blacks or deep blues.

The first essential is that the colours chosen should be transparent. These will generally be indicated in most makers' lists and can include such colours as French ultramarine, cobalt, viridian, rose madder and alizarin crimson.

Although the field of glazing is sadly neglected by many painters, perhaps because the preparatory work must first be left for a period to dry out thoroughly, yet it can be one of the most rewarding of practices, and once the principles and the methods are understood, the glazes can be taken into consideration when a picture is being planned. The vehicles for glazing are

Glazing

54

Bideford Bridge by the author. The lower half of the river and the reflections are put in by several layers of glazing various. They can be oils, such as linseed or poppy, or varnishes, such as the natural resins, copal, dammar and mastic. If greater fluidity is required, all these glazes can be diluted with white spirit, but this should not be greater than one part of white spirit to one part of oil, varnish or medium.

The brush chosen should have a long head and hold liquid colour well; a hair brush is likely to produce a more even finish than a bristle. Unless the glaze is for a very small area, it is best mixed in a saucer or a ceramic well-palette. Before applying the glaze, make quite sure the colour is thoroughly and evenly dispersed in the vehicle; if this is not watched, unpleasant streaks will appear on the area treated.

Depending on the size of the area being glazed, the picture can be left vertical on the easel or laid with a slight tilt on a table. Treat the application just as though it were a matter of putting on a watercolour wash. Start at the top and allow the liquid colour to flow evenly down. Be as direct as possible and avoid going back over an area, as this can lead to unevenness. When the bottom is reached, remove any excess colour.

Graded glazing can be attempted by increasing the amount of pigment or vehicle. Intentional 'bleeding' of one colour into another is also quite possible and can offer exciting results. It will be found that the alkyd colours will answer most satisfactorily for any type of glazing, and they will evince a greater degree of fluidity and control than is found with the conventional oil colours.

Other methods for applying a transparent colour film include stippling straight down on to the canvas with a large round hog-hair brush, dabbing on the glaze with a pad or rag wrapped round a wad of cotton wool, or working into a previously laid wet glaze with a scrap of clean dry rag or a clean brush. With these methods it is possible to adjust the strength of the colour to a high degree of subtlety.

In thinking out the possibilities for exploiting the glaze technique, bear in mind the effect of light coming through stained glass windows. When you glaze you are virtually putting a transparent colour on top of an opaque colour, and this latter will be transformed – a degree of translucence will be produced, making the area 'sing' with a contained richness.

Often, previously unthought of combinations can result in stimulating effects. Alizarin crimson over a bright green (mixed from lamp black and cadmium yellow) will produce a moss-like green of great depth. French ultramarine or cobalt over cadmium yellow or yellow ochre will give a range of limpid wet greens – useful for water reflections or luscious foliage. Cadmium red over raw sienna and cadmium yellow gives a flame-like quality. Viridian over cadmium red can produce a brown, warm and deep.

The combinations are legion and each will have its own individual variations, depending upon the strength of the glaze used.

Velatura

Closely allied to glazing is a manner called *velatura* which was used by a number of the painters of the Renaissance. This involved mixing small quantities of certain transparent colours with varnish. This mixture would then be brushed over the whole surface of a finished and well-dried painting, the idea being that this tinted varnish film would 'take down' the brightness of certain passages, but at the same time give prominence to some details.

Scumbling

This is the opposite of glazing and, in brief, consists of the placing of opaque colours over a wet or dry underpainting in such a way that something of the first painting makes its presence felt through the opaque layer. The result can be one of softness, a toning down of a passage, producing an effect of mistiness.

The scumbling can be done by applying the opaque colour with a fingertip or a piece of rag and rubbing it out over the area. A form of scumble can be to use a fairly wide, flat hog brush, lightly load it with the chosen colour, and then, holding the brush nearly flat to the canvas, drag it across leaving a thin broken layer of colour over the underpainting.

The opaque colours used may be put on stiff as they come from the tube or they can be diluted with one or other of the vehicles suggested in the foregoing section on glazing.

Rubbing

Although this may appear to be close to scumbling, it is in fact different. It is the manipulation of the paints on the canvas by rubbing with the fingers, thumbs, knuckles and palm of the hand, but without the express purpose of achieving an effect from an underpainting. Many painters use this method for manipulation; it may be just to achieve a small blend of a feature in a portrait by the flick of the tip of a little finger, or it can be the softening of an outline with the thumb or the smoothing down of a passage with a sweep of the palm of the hand.

'Tonking'

A device reputedly thought of by Henry Tonks, the great teacher from the Slade School, London. When a painting has been repeatedly worked at and

Goose Fair by the author
(Private Collection).
Painted over an alizarin
crimson imprimatura
and with considerable
use of scumbling

the colours have become thicker and thicker, so that the resulting image has moved far away from the original intention, it may sometimes be rescued for a fresh attempt, by 'tonking'. A piece of greaseproof or similar paper is laid over the whole face of the painting whilst the paint is still wet and gently smoothed down with the palm of the hand. It is then peeled off, bringing with it much of the excess colour. The remains on the canvas can often be reworked so that the lost design, intention, and freshness are recaptured.

Varnishing

This is an essential last step if a painting is to be preserved. Oil paintings need the shield of a good stable varnish if they are to survive the effects of atmosphere with humidity, dust and the rest; the more so in an industrial environment where pollution is heavy and cannot possibly be kept from the paint films. Putting oil paintings behind glass is not a real solution, for, unless they are hermetically sealed in, the pollutants can still attack. Even if the sealing is complete, glass is still not a good idea, because some damp may have been trapped inside and any mould spores present can grow.

Furthermore, a coat of varnish can bring back to the colours that state of brilliance seen by the painter as he puts the finishing strokes to the picture.

The different types of varnish were discussed on p. 23. The principal point to remember is that varnishing should not be done until the picture has dried out completely; a safe period to wait is about 12 months. If it is imperative to varnish earlier (such as when a picture must be shown in an exhibition), this may be done, provided the surface is skin-dry, using retouching varnish.

As far as possible, final varnishing should be carried out on a dry day. Try to do it in as dust-free an atmosphere as possible. Before commencing, dust off the surface using a large soft brush. If there should be any areas where grime persists, these may be treated by applying very gently a brush slightly moistened with the minimum of white spirit. Allow this to dry thoroughly before proceeding.

Whether the picture is placed vertically on the easel or laid flat on a table is a matter for personal choice. Some of the selected varnish should be poured out into a saucer and used with a flat, white, hog-bristle brush. Be careful not to pick up too much. Starting at the top of the picture and using a system of short strokes from different angles, work your way over the picture, aiming to lay a thin even film. Have the canvas set against the light, so that it is easy to see if any areas have been missed and if too much varnish has been put on, causing 'runs' or trickles to form.

Apple Trees in Flower at Pontoise, Pissaro (*Christie's*). Here is the broken colour effect so much used by the Impressionists

The varnished painting should be left for at least six hours to allow for hardening; if natural resin varnishes are being used the time should be doubled. For further safety, the picture should really be left for three or four days to become completely hard before framing, otherwise sticking can occur where there is the pressure from the edge of the frame.

Framing

A picture needs a frame to bring it to life. For oils it is generally better not to use glass, as the paintings will then be easier to see and appreciate. As to the type of frame, it will largely be a question of personal preference. A local frame-maker will generally have a reasonable selection of mouldings from which to choose. With his advice, try to get a width that will balance with the size of the painting. Avoid overshadowing a small picture with a very wide and ornate frame – a mistake that often happened in the nineteenth century.

The perfect frame should complement the painting. In its design and finish and general tones, it should act as a harmonious container and assist in bringing out the values of the painting.

Sometimes the appearance of a picture when in the frame can be enhanced by the insertion of a fillet (an inner border). This can be easily made with strips of strong card which have had lengths of toned linen or raw canvas stuck on to them.

An economical approach to framing can be to visit a timber merchant and buy some lengths of standard joinery mouldings which he will undoubtedly stock. These can be glazing strips, picture rails, architrave or door panel mouldings. From such can be built up attractive frame mouldings for a fraction of the cost of standard types; basing the frame on lengths of two-by-one deal. The ornamental strips can be glued and fixed into place with panel pins.

The finish can be in a variety of ways; the simplest being a toning with emulsion paint. A more complicated scheme which will provide quality appearance can be to brush on a layer of gesso – a mixture of whiting and water-soluble glue. This should be prepared to the consistency of clotted cream and heated in a double saucepan. The gesso may be applied fairly thin and given a stippled look by dabbing with the brush or put on quite thick and then given a more robust texture. This latter can be done using a comb, either in a straight down manner or criss-cross pattern. You can also cut out various toothed designs on the edges of pieces of stiff cardboard which can widen the scope of texture making.

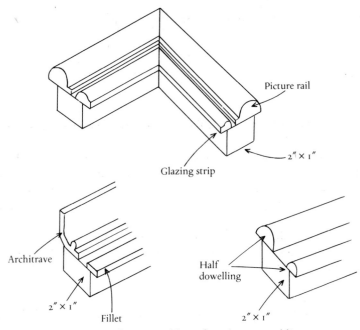

Picture rail

2″ × 1″

Glazing strip

Architrave

2″ × 1″

Fillet

Half
dowelling

2″ × 1″

Building up frame mouldings from house mouldings

The gesso should then be left to harden out for at least forty-eight hours. After that, rough or unwanted upstanding pieces should be sanded down.

To prepare the final finish, make up a saturated solution of shellac in alcohol or prepare a fairly strong size. One of these is necessary to isolate the gesso which is very absorbent. If you are going to 'gild' the frame the effect can be enriched by first brushing over the isolated gesso a thin imprimatura of light red with a little burnt umber. Most gold frames today are not covered with gold leaf but with an artificial gold paint. Various tones of this liquid can be bought or you can make up your own by purchasing some bronze powder with the tint that you need and then mixing it to a brushing consistency with cellulose or acrylic medium. Permanence will be increased if after it is dry a coat of picture varnish is applied.

If an 'antique' effect is sought, the preparation will take a little longer. Step one is to dab at random over the frame weak splodges of green, blue, umber and red oil colours, diluted with turpentine substitute. Leave for twenty-four hours and then paint over with a light-toned distemper – somewhere around porridge colour – and while this is still moist, lightly wipe off small areas here and there, which will expose some of the

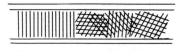

Regular and random combing into moist gesso

underlying colours and the gilding. Again, leave for twenty-four hours and as a last step apply a little good quality wax furniture polish, either in paste or liquid form and buff up with a pad of rags or cotton wool.

When you fit the picture into the frame, fix it in place with small brass plates, which are sold in ironmongers and generally called 'shelf-ears'. These should be screwed to the frame only – never on to a stretcher or a panel, as this could cause damage, and in any case the picture should not be rigidly held in place and should have room to move. These small brass plates are far more satisfactory than nails which are hammered into the frame and then bent over to hold the picture; a worse sin is that sometimes the nails are hammered right through the stretcher and can be exceedingly difficult to remove without causing damage. Further, banging nails into an old gilt-gesso frame is almost certain to crack the gesso.

Screw-eyes or hanging-plates to take the cord or the chains should be placed about a third of the way down the frame. This will allow a picture to hang with a slight tilt forwards. Not only will the picture then be easier to see when it is on the wall, but this will also prevent dust falling on to the surface of a painting.

A final caution – don't take it for granted that even stout hanging cords, wires or chains will last forever. In damp conditions they can perish and rot

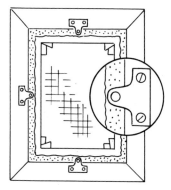

Fixing picture in frame with 'shelf-ears'

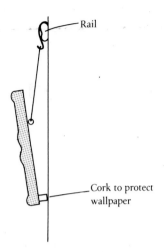

Rail

Cork to protect
wallpaper

Correct way to hang a picture

quite quickly. Get into the habit of an annual inspection; it can save you from a crash in the night and perhaps even a tear in a canvas or a wrecked frame.